Sanjeev Kapoor's

MONSOON Medley

In association with Alyona Kapoor

Popular Prakashan
www.popularprakashan.com

Published by
POPULAR PRAKASHAN PVT. LTD.
301, Mahalaxmi Chambers
22, Bhulabhai Desai Road
Mumbai - 400 026
for Khana Khazana Publications Pvt. Ltd.

First Published 2010
Third Reprint November 2011

(4354)
ISBN: 978-81-7991-606-3

Design: Mahendra Ghanekar & Anjali Sawant
Photography: Bharat Bhirangi & Alim Bolar

PRINTED IN INDIA
by Trident Offset Works
B-97/4, Naraina Industrial Area
Phase I, New Delhi

Author's Note

Enjoy the rains with this lip-smacking medley of monsoon recipes!

The pitter-patter of raindrops on the window pane, the warm fragrance of the rain drenching the dry and parched earth, the cold grey skies are signals to indulge your inner malhar!

Curl up on your favourite sofa, sipping on piping hot *Masala Chai*, tangy *Tomato Saar* or zesty Lemon Pepper Soup, a plate of crispy crunchy Potato Fingers close at hand. Welcome every shower of rain with your favourite monsoon comfort foods like classic

Bhuna Bhutta, spicy *Mirchi Bhajiya*, and tempting *Missal Pav*.

Transform your grey monsoon mood with this rainbow of delights which is guaranteed to brighten up a rainy day!

Happy Cooking!

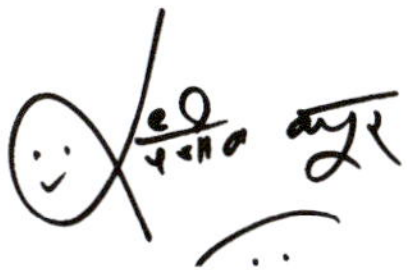

Contents

Masala Chai

4-6 teaspoons tea leaves

1 cup milk

1 teaspoon *Chai Masala* (see below)

4 teaspoons sugar

- Boil three cups of water in a non-stick pan. Add the tea leaves, milk, *chai masala* and sugar and bring the mixture to a boil again. Boil for a couple of minutes.
- Strain and serve piping hot.

Chai Masala

Dry-roast and grind 1 inch cinnamon, 4 green cardamoms, 16 black peppercorns and ¼ teaspoon grated nutmeg. Sift the powder and store in an airtight container.

Filter Coffee

3 tablespoons freshly ground-coffee powder

4 cups milk

2 tablespoons sugar

- Bring one cup of water to a boil in a non-stick pan.
- Add the coffee powder in the upper chamber of a filter-coffee maker.
- Pour the boiling water over the coffee powder; cover and set aside to let the water filter through the powder.
- Heat the milk till it comes to a boil. Pour the milk into four cups and add sugar to taste.
- Pour the coffee decoction into the cups and stir. Serve at once.

Irish Coffee

½ cup Irish whiskey, or Irish mint liqueur

2 teaspoons instant coffee powder

4 teaspoons sugar

¼ cup heavy cream, chilled

- Add two teaspoons of sugar to the chilled cream and whip till it forms soft peaks. Set aside.
- Pour three cups of water into a deep microwave-safe bowl. Cover and cook on HIGH (100%) for five minutes or until steaming.
- Add the coffee powder and the remaining two teaspoons of sugar. Stir to dissolve.
- Gradually pour in the whiskey or liqueur.
- Pour the coffee into four stemmed glasses and top with whipped cream.

Kahwa

1 teaspoon *kahwa* tea leaves, crushed

2 green cardamoms

2 inches cinnamon

3 teaspoons sugar, or to taste

2-3 saffron threads (optional)

4-5 almonds, finely ground

- Pound the cardamoms and cinnamon to a powder.
- Pour three cups of water into a non-stick pan. Add the crushed *kahwa* tea leaves, sugar, cardamom-cinnamon powder and saffron. Bring to a boil.
- Boil for five to six minutes till the tea turns light golden.
- Strain into tea cups.
- Sprinkle with the ground almonds and serve hot.

Badam Doodh

60 almonds, blanched and peeled

8 cups milk

A generous pinch of saffron

½ teaspoon green cardamom powder

A pinch of nutmeg powder

12 tablespoons sugar

- Slice fifteen almonds and grind the rest to a paste.
- Bring the milk to a boil in a thick-bottomed non-stick pan.
- Lower heat, add the almond paste and simmer for fifteen to twenty minutes.
- Add the saffron, cardamom powder, nutmeg powder and sugar, and mix well.
- Pour into individual glasses, garnish with sliced almonds and serve hot.

Sabzi Ka Shorba

3 medium potatoes, cut into ½-inch cubes

3 large tomatoes, chopped

100 grams bottle gourd, cut into ½-inch cubes

2 tablespoons oil

5-6 black peppercorns

2 cloves

2 onions, chopped

2 garlic cloves, crushed

1 inch ginger, chopped

3 cups Vegetable Stock (page 95)

¼ teaspoon turmeric powder

Salt to taste

½ teaspoon sugar

½ teaspoon black pepper powder

1 tablespoon lemon juice

1 spring onion, chopped

- Heat the oil in a deep non-stick pan; add the peppercorns and cloves, and sauté for half a minute. Add the onions and cook over medium heat till translucent.
- Add the garlic and ginger, and stir. Add the potatoes, tomatoes and bottle gourd, and cook over

medium heat for five minutes, stirring occasionally.

- Add the vegetable stock, turmeric powder, salt, sugar and pepper powder. Increase the heat and bring the soup to a boil.
- Lower the heat and simmer for about thirty minutes, or till the vegetables are tender. Cool and purée in a blender. Pass the purée through a strainer.
- Return the purée to the pan, add the lemon juice, and bring the soup to a boil. Serve hot, garnished with the chopped spring onion.

Spinach And Potato Soup

30 spinach leaves, finely chopped

3 medium potatoes, boiled and mashed

1 medium onion, finely chopped

4 cups Vegetable Stock (page 95)

Salt to taste

½ teaspoon black pepper powder

½ cup skimmed milk

- Heat a deep non-stick pan. Add the onion and roast for a couple of minutes taking care that the colour of onion does not change.
- Add the vegetable stock and bring it to a boil.
- Add the potatoes and mix well. Add the spinach and cook till the leaves are tender. Add salt to taste and the pepper powder.
- Add the milk and bring it to a boil.
- Serve piping hot.

Paneer And Lemon Grass Soup

200 grams cottage cheese, cut into ½-inch cubes

1 inch lemon grass, chopped

1 teaspoon oil

3 garlic cloves, chopped

4-5 cups Vegetable Stock (page 95)

1 fresh red chilli, sliced

Salt to taste

A pinch of MSG (optional)

½ tablespoon lemon juice

2-3 stalks spring onion greens, sliced

- Heat the oil in a non-stick wok; add the garlic and sauté over medium heat for half a minute. Add the lemon grass and continue to sauté for half a minute.
- Add the vegetable stock and bring to a boil. Lower the heat, add the red chilli, salt and MSG, and simmer, uncovered, for five minutes, stirring occasionally.
- Add the cottage cheese and lemon juice, stir and continue to simmer for one minute.
- Ladle the soup into individual serving bowls, garnish with spring onion greens and serve hot.

Vegetable Noodle Soup

4-5 fresh button mushrooms, finely sliced

1 medium carrot, grated

½ medium green capsicum, cut into thin strips

8-10 spinach leaves, finely shredded

40 grams eggless noodles

1 tablespoon oil

2-3 garlic cloves, crushed

1 dried red chilli, seeded and finely chopped

4-5 cups Vegetable Stock (page 95)

¼ teaspoon MSG (optional)

¼ teaspoon white pepper powder

Salt to taste

1 tablespoon white vinegar

- Heat the oil in a non-stick pan; add the garlic and stir-fry for half a minute.
- Add the mushrooms, carrot and capsicum, and stir-fry for two minutes.
- Add the red chilli and immediately stir in the stock. Bring the mixture to a boil.

- Add the noodles; lower the heat and simmer for three to four minutes, stirring occasionally.
- Add the MSG, white pepper powder and salt to taste.
- Stir in the vinegar and shredded spinach leaves, cook for one minute and serve hot.

Chef's Tip

Vary the quantity of noodles to taste. To make a complete meal of this soup, increase the quantity of noodles and serve in a large bowl.

Vegetable Manchow Soup

2-3 dried Chinese mushrooms

2 slices bamboo shoot

1 spring onion with greens

2-3 fresh button mushrooms, finely chopped

¼ small cabbage, finely chopped

50 grams bean curd (tofu), finely chopped

1 medium capsicum, finely chopped

1 medium carrot, finely diced

1 cup noodles

2 tablespoons oil + for deep-frying

½ inch fresh ginger, peeled and finely chopped

2-3 garlic cloves, peeled and finely chopped

2 green chillies, chopped

½ tablespoon red chilli sauce

2 tablespoons soy sauce

½ teaspoon white pepper powder

¼ teaspoon MSG (optional)

Salt to taste

4-5 cups Vegetable Stock (page 95)

3 tablespoons cornflour

1 tablespoon vinegar

- Wash and soak the Chinese mushrooms in hot water for fifteen minutes. Drain, wash thoroughly and chop fine.
- Boil the bamboo shoot slices in half a cup of water for three to four minutes. Drain, cool and chop fine. Finely chop the spring onion, reserving some chopped spring onion greens for garnishing.
- Boil the noodles in three cups of hot water and spread on a plate to dry.
- Heat sufficient oil in a non-stick wok and deep-fry the boiled noodles for two to three minutes, or until light brown and crisp. Remove and drain on absorbent paper.
- Heat two tablespoons of oil in a non-stick pan; add the chopped ginger, garlic and green chillies, and stir-fry for a few seconds. Add the chopped spring onion, and cook for a couple of minutes.
- Add the chopped bamboo shoots, mushrooms, cabbage, bean curd, capsicum and carrot, and cook on medium heat, stirring continuously for two minutes.
- Add the chilli sauce, soy sauce, white pepper powder, MSG and salt to

taste, and stir well to mix. Stir in the vegetable stock and bring to a boil. Lower heat and simmer for two to three minutes.

- Mix the cornflour and half a cup of water, stir into the soup and cook for two minutes or until the soup thickens, stirring continuously.

- Stir in the vinegar and serve piping hot, garnished with crisp fried noodles and the reserved spring onion greens.

Garlic Rasam

15-20 garlic cloves, roasted

2 tablespoons split pigeon peas, soaked

1 medium tomato, cubed

2 teaspoons Tamarind Pulp (page 95)

Salt to taste

A pinch of asafoetida

¼ teaspoon turmeric powder

Rasam Powder

1 teaspoon cumin seeds

6-8 black peppercorns

4 dried red chillies

1 tablespoon coriander seeds

1 teaspoon split Bengal gram

Seasoning

½ teaspoon mustard seeds

2 dried red chillies

1 sprig curry leaves

- Boil three cups of water in a deep non-stick pan. Add the split pigeon peas and tomato cubes and cook, covered, till soft. Mash and reserve along with the water.

- For the *rasam* powder, in a non-stick pan, dry-roast the cumin seeds, peppercorns, whole red chillies, coriander seeds and split Bengal gram till light brown. Cool and pound to a powder.
- Add three cups of water to the tamarind pulp and boil it with the salt, asafoetida, turmeric powder and *masala* powder for five minutes.
- Add the mashed pigeon peas to the *rasam* and bring it to a boil. Lower the heat and simmer for five minutes. Strain and bring to a boil again.
- For the seasoning, dry-roast the mustard seeds, red chillies and curry leaves in a non-stick pan and add it to the boiling *rasam*. Cover immediately to trap the flavours and serve piping hot garnished with roasted garlic.

Chef's Tip

You can pound the garlic very lightly before adding for a stronger flavour. You can also pressure-cook the garlic separately and then add it to the *rasam*. Increase or decrease the quantity of garlic to taste.

Tomato Rasam

2 medium tomatoes, chopped

4 tablespoons split pigeon peas

½ lemon-sized ball tamarind

¼ cup chopped fresh coriander

1½ teaspoons Rasam Powder (page 24)

¼ teaspoon asafoetida

Salt to taste

10-12 curry leaves

4 tablespoons pure ghee

½ teaspoon mustard seeds

2 dried red chillies

- Wash, drain and cook the split pigeon peas in two cups of water until soft. Strain and mash well. Reserve the strained cooking liquid.
- Soak the tamarind in one cup of warm water; squeeze out the pulp, strain and reserve.
- Reserve some chopped coriander for garnishing. Mix the tamarind pulp with the remaining coriander, *rasam* powder, asafoetida, salt and half the quantity of curry leaves. Bring to a boil, lower the heat and simmer for two or three minutes.

- Add the chopped tomatoes and the reserved cooking liquid. Simmer for four or five minutes and stir in the mashed pigeon peas and cook for another minute.

- Remove from the heat and sprinkle the reserved chopped coriander.

- Heat the ghee in a small non-stick pan; add the mustard seeds and sauté till they begin to splutter.

- Add the red chillies and the remaining curry leaves and stir well.

- Pour the sizzling spices over the *rasam* and cover immediately to trap the flavours. Serve hot.

Chef's Tip

To serve *rasam* as an appetiser, strain and pour into small glasses, garnished with a slice of lemon. Traditionally, *rasam* is cooked in a pan made from a special alloy, which gives the *rasam* its unique flavour.

Tomato Saar

5-6 large ripe tomatoes, roughly chopped

1 cup grated coconut

6 garlic cloves

1 teaspoon cumin seeds

Salt to taste

½ teaspoon red chilli powder

2 tablespoons ghee

1 teaspoon mustard seeds

A pinch of asafoetida

8-10 curry leaves

3-4 green chillies, slit into two

2-3 tablespoons sugar

¼ cup chopped fresh coriander

- Grind together the grated coconut, garlic and cumin seeds to a paste.
- In a non-stick pan, mix together the tomatoes, salt, chilli powder and three cups of water, and bring it to a boil.
- Simmer for fifteen minutes and purée when cooled slightly. Heat the ghee in a non-stick pan; add the mustard seeds, asafoetida and curry leaves. When the mustard

seeds begin to splutter, add the puréed tomatoes and slit green chillies and bring to a boil.

- Stir in the sugar and the coconut-spice paste.
- Cook on a low heat for ten minutes.
- Serve hot, garnished with chopped coriander.

Lemon Pepper Soup

1½ tablespoons lemon juice

3 black peppercorns, crushed

¾ teaspoon oil

¾ tablespoon gram flour

¾ medium carrot, grated

¼ small cabbage, finely shredded

4 fresh button mushrooms, sliced

½ medium green capsicum, chopped

½ medium tomato, finely chopped

Salt to taste

3-4 cups Vegetable Stock (page 95)

½ cup bean sprouts

- Heat the oil in a non-stick pan; add the gram flour and stir-fry for a few seconds.
- Add the carrot, cabbage and mushrooms, and stir to mix.
- Add the capsicum, tomato and salt, and stir-fry for one minute.
- Add the vegetable stock and bring to a boil; simmer for two to three minutes.
- Add the crushed peppercorns and remove from the heat. Stir in the bean sprouts and the lemon juice, and serve piping hot.

Mushroom Soup With Light Soy

30 grams fresh button mushrooms

3 cups Vegetable Stock (page 95)

1 teaspoon light soy sauce

150 grams silken bean curd (tofu), finely diced

Salt to taste

½ teaspoon black pepper powder

4 teaspoons sliced spring onions

- Pour the vegetable stock and light soy sauce in a deep non-stick pan and bring the mixture to a boil.
- Add the mushrooms and bean curd, and cook over low heat for three to four minutes, but do not allow the mixture to boil. Add the salt and pepper powder. Stir to mix well.
- Ladle the soup into individual soup bowls, and garnish with a teaspoon of spring onions on top, and serve piping hot.

Curried Cauliflower Soup

1 medium cauliflower, separated into small florets

1 medium potato, cut into small pieces

Salt to taste

1½ teaspoons oil

1 medium onion, finely chopped

½ inch ginger, finely chopped

4 garlic cloves, finely chopped

4 cups Vegetable Stock (page 95)

½ teaspoons cumin seeds

¼ teaspoons mustard seeds

½ teaspoons turmeric powder

2 teaspoons coriander powder

1 cup yogurt

½ cup milk

2 teaspoons gram flour

A few sprigs of fresh coriander, chopped

- Soak separately the cauliflower florets and the potato pieces in salted water.
- Heat one teaspoon oil in a thick-bottomed non-stick pan; add the chopped onion and sauté for two minutes. Add the chopped ginger

and garlic and sauté for another two minutes. Drain and add the potato.

- Drain and add the cauliflower and stir on high heat for three to four minutes.
- Stir in two cups of vegetable stock and bring to a boil. Cover and simmer till the cauliflower and potatoes are cooked.
- Remove from the heat and cool the mixture. Purée the cauliflower and potato mixture in a blender.
- Heat half a teaspoon of oil and add the cumin seeds and mustard seeds.
- When the mustard seeds start to splutter, add the cauliflower and potato purée along with the remaining vegetable stock. Mix well and cook on low heat. Add the turmeric powder, and coriander powder and mix well.
- Whisk the yogurt and milk in a bowl. Add the gram flour and continue to whisk till smooth. Stir the mixture into the soup and cook for a while. Season with salt if required.
- Serve hot, garnished with chopped coriander.

Sweetcorn Soup With Mixed Vegetables And Tofu

150 grams cream-style sweetcorn

½ cup sweetcorn kernels

¼ small cabbage, chopped

¼ medium carrot, chopped

100 grams bean curd (tofu), cut into ½-inch pieces

2 tablespoons oil

4-5 cups Vegetable Stock (page 95)

Salt to taste

¼ teaspoon white pepper powder

½ tablespoon sugar

¼ teaspoon MSG (optional)

3 tablespoons cornflour

1 stalk spring onion greens, chopped

- Heat the oil in a non-stick wok; add the corn, cabbage and carrot, and stir-fry for two minutes. Stir in the vegetable stock and bring to a boil.
- Mix in the cream-style corn and continue to cook for two to three minutes.

- Add the salt, white pepper powder, sugar and MSG. Add the bean curd and stir in the cornflour, mixed with half a cup of water.
- Cook over high heat, stirring continuously, for one minute, or until the soup thickens.
- Serve piping hot, garnished with spring onion greens.

Dahi Shorba

1 cup yogurt
2 teaspoons gram flour
1-2 green chillies, chopped
1 inch ginger, chopped
¼ teaspoon sugar
Salt to taste
2 teaspoons ghee
1 teaspoon cumin seeds
1 medium carrot, finely chopped
4-6 French beans, finely chopped
2 tablespoons green peas
1 medium green capsicum, finely chopped
5-6 small cauliflower florets, finely chopped

- Grind the green chillies and the ginger to a fine paste. Whisk the yogurt with three cups of water. Add the gram flour, green chilli-ginger paste, sugar and salt, and mix well. Heat the ghee in a thick-bottomed non-stick pan; add the cumin seeds and stir-fry until light golden brown.

- Add the chopped carrot, beans, peas, capsicum and cauliflower. Sauté the vegetables for two or three minutes. Stir in the yogurt mixture and bring to a boil; lower the heat and simmer for eight to ten minutes, or until thick. Adjust the seasoning and serve hot.

Mini Uttappa With Aloo Bhaji

2 cups ready-mixed *uttappam* batter

Oil as required

½ cup *aloo bhaji*

8 tablespoons grated mozzarella cheese

2 teaspoons Red Chilli-Garlic Chutney (page 94)

4 teaspoons Green Chutney (page 94)

4 teaspoons Date and Tamarind Chutney (page 94)

6 tablespoons *sev*

- Heat a non-stick *tawa* and grease it lightly. For each *uttappam*, pour one ladleful of batter onto the *tawa* and spread with the back of the ladle to make a moderately thick three-inch round *uttappam*. Drizzle some oil all around.

- Spread a little *aloo bhaji* on top and cook till the bottom of the *uttappam* is pale gold. Sprinkle the mozzarella cheese over the *bhaji*, cover the *tawa* and cook till the cheese melts.

- Remove the cover and turn out the *uttappam* onto a serving plate. Spread all the three chutneys over the top, sprinkle *sev* and serve immediately.

Pav Bhaji

8 *pav*

4 medium potatoes, boiled and grated

4 medium tomatoes, finely chopped

1 medium green capsicum, chopped

¼ cup shelled green peas, boiled and mashed lightly

¼ small cauliflower, grated

3 tablespoons oil

2 medium onions, finely chopped

3-4 green chillies, finely chopped

2 teaspoons ginger paste

2 teaspoons garlic paste

1½ tablespoons *pav bhaji masala*

Salt to taste

3 tablespoons butter

2 tablespoons finely chopped fresh coriander

2 lemons, cut into wedges

- Heat the oil in a non-stick pan; add three-fourth of the onions and sauté till light brown.
- Add the green chillies, ginger paste and garlic paste, and stir-fry for half a minute.

- Add half the tomatoes and cook over medium heat, stirring continuously, for three to four minutes, or till the oil separates.

- Add the capsicum, peas, cauliflower, potatoes and one and a half cups of water. Bring to a boil, lower heat and simmer for ten minutes, mashing the vegetables with the back of the spoon a few times, till all the vegetables are completely mashed.

- Add the *pav bhaji masala*, salt and the remaining tomatoes. Cook over medium heat for two minutes, stirring continuously.

- Heat half the butter in a thick-bottomed non-stick pan or a *tawa*. Cut the *pav* horizontally into two and fry in butter, pressing down two or three times, for half a minute, or till the *pav* is crisp and light brown.

- Garnish the *bhaji* with the chopped coriander and remaining butter, and serve hot with *pav*, the remaining onions and lemon wedges.

Bhuna Bhutta

2 American corn cobs

Salt to taste

2 tablespoons butter

2 tablespoons lemon juice

1 teaspoon red chilli flakes (optional)

1 teaspoon red chilli powder (optional)

2 teaspoons brown sugar (optional)

- Remove the husks from the corn.
- Place each cob on a twelve-inch square piece of aluminium foil.
- Either sprinkle with salt and brush with butter and lemon juice, or sprinkle salt, chilli flakes, chilli powder and brown sugar and brush with butter and lemon juice.
- Wrap the corn in aluminium foil and twist the ends to seal. Place on live charcoal or on a grill and cook for fifteen minutes.
- Open the foil wrapping and serve hot.

Sabudana Vada

1½ cups sago

3 medium potatoes, boiled and mashed

1 cup roasted peanuts, coarsely ground

3 green chillies, finely chopped

2 tablespoons chopped fresh coriander

1 tablespoon lemon juice

Salt to taste

Oil for frying

- Soak the sago in enough water to cover it, for about two hours. Drain out the excess water.
- Mix together the sago, mashed potatoes, ground peanuts, chopped green chillies, chopped coriander, lemon juice and salt. Mix thoroughly.
- Divide into sixteen portions and shape into lemon-sized balls, flatten between your palms and deep-fry in hot oil till golden brown.
- Serve hot with chutney.

Paneer Koliwada

300 grams cottage cheese

½ cup gram flour

½ teaspoon cumin powder

2 teaspoons Kashmiri red chilli powder

Salt to taste

1 tablespoon ginger paste

1 tablespoon garlic paste

2 tablespoons yogurt

2 tablespoons lemon juice

Oil for deep-frying

½ teaspoon *chaat masala*

- Cut the cottage cheese into three-inch by half-inch by half-inch pieces. Mix together the gram flour, cumin powder, chilli powder, salt, ginger paste, garlic paste, yogurt, lemon juice and a little water if necessary, into a thick batter.
- Marinate the cottage cheese in the batter for half an hour. Heat sufficient oil in a non-stick *kadai* and deep-fry the cottage cheese till crisp on the outside. Serve hot, sprinkled with *chaat masala.*

Chef's Tip

To make *paneer koliwada* extra crisp, add a tablespoon of cornflour to the batter.

Aloo Ki Tikki

6 medium potatoes, boiled and mashed

Salt to taste

1 tablespoon oil + for deep-frying

1 medium onion, chopped

¼ cup grated cottage cheese

¼ cup chopped fresh coriander

6-8 cashew nuts, crushed

½ tablespoon red chilli powder

- Add salt to the mashed potatoes and knead into a smooth dough. Divide into twelve equal portions.
- Heat one tablespoon of oil in a non-stick pan and sauté the onion till translucent. Cool and mix with the cottage cheese, chopped coriander, cashew nuts, chilli powder and salt. Divide the mixture into twelve equal portions.
- Stuff each portion of mashed potato with a portion of the cottage cheese mixture. Roll and shape into a half-inch thick, two-inch round *tikki*.
- Heat the oil in a non-stick *kadai* and deep-fry the *tikki* till golden brown. Drain on absorbent paper.
- Serve hot with tomato ketchup or chutney.

Crispy Wontons

24 Wonton Wrappers (page 95)

2 tablespoons oil + for deep-frying

4-6 garlic cloves, chopped

2 spring onions, chopped

2 medium green capsicums, chopped

8-10 French beans, chopped

2 medium carrots, chopped

½ small cabbage, chopped

½ teaspoon white pepper powder

Salt to taste

¼ teaspoon MSG (optional)

1 teaspoon soy sauce

- For the filling, heat two tablespoons of oil in a non-stick wok or a pan; add the garlic and stir-fry for half a minute. Add the spring onions and capsicums, French beans, carrots and cabbage, and continue to stir-fry for a couple of minutes longer, stirring and tossing continuously.

- Add the white pepper powder, salt, MSG and soy sauce, and cook for half a minute. Remove from the heat and cool.

- Divide the prepared filling into twenty-four equal portions. Place a portion of the filling in the centre of each wonton wrapper, moisten the edges with a little water, fold in half diagonally, twist the ends and press lightly to stick together.

- Heat sufficient oil in a non-stick wok and deep-fry the wontons for two to three minutes, or until crisp and golden brown.
- Drain on absorbent paper.
- Serve hot with Sichuan Sauce (page 95).

Note: *You can use ready-made wonton wrappers.*

Corn Pakore

250 grams fresh corn kernels

2 teaspoons green chilli paste

1½ teaspoons ginger paste

1 teaspoon *chaat masala*

1 teaspoon coriander powder

2 tablespoons chopped fresh coriander

5-6 tablespoons gram flour

Salt to taste

Oil for deep-frying

- Coarsely grind the corn and place in a large bowl. Add the green chilli paste, ginger paste, *chaat masala*, coriander powder, chopped coriander, gram flour and salt. Mix well.

- Heat sufficient oil in a non-stick *kadai*. Drop small portions of the corn mixture into the hot oil and deep-fry the *pakore* till golden brown on both sides. Drain on absorbent paper.

- Serve hot with Green Chutney (page 94).

Crunchy Paneer

300 grams cottage cheese, cut into 1-inch cubes

¼ cup refined flour

1 tablespoon oil + for deep-frying

½ inch ginger, chopped

2 garlic cloves, chopped

¼ celery stalk, chopped

Salt to taste

5-6 black peppercorns, crushed

A small pinch of MSG (optional)

½ tablespoon dark soy sauce

½ teaspoon sugar

1 teaspoon vinegar

2 stalks spring onion greens, sliced

Batter

¾ cup cornflour

6 tablespoons refined flour

½ teaspoon baking powder

Salt to taste

- Dust the cottage cheese cubes with refined flour. Mix together all the ingredients for the batter together with three-fourth cup plus one and a half tablespoons of chilled water and whisk with a balloon whisk till smooth.

- Heat sufficient oil in a non-stick wok. Dip the cottage cheese cubes in the batter and deep-fry till golden and crisp. Drain on absorbent paper.
- Heat one tablespoon of oil in a non-stick wok; add the ginger and the garlic and sauté over medium heat for half a minute.
- Add the celery and continue to sauté for half a minute more.
- Add the fried cottage cheese cubes, salt, crushed peppercorns, MSG, soy sauce, sugar and vinegar, and cook over high heat for one minute, stirring and tossing continuously.
- Serve hot, garnished with spring onion greens.

Hare Matar Aur Paneer Ke Shaami Kabab

½ cup shelled green peas, coarsely ground

350 grams cottage cheese

300 grams yam, boiled and mashed

1 tablespoon oil + for shallow-frying

1 teaspoon cumin seeds

1 inch ginger, chopped

6 green chillies, chopped

Salt to taste

2 tablespoons chopped fresh coriander

¼ teaspoon turmeric powder

1 teaspoon *garam masala* powder

1½ teaspoons red chilli powder

½ teaspoon *chaat masala*

½ teaspoon dried mango powder

2 tablespoons cornflour

Green Chutney (page 94)

- Grate the cottage cheese and knead till smooth.
- Heat one tablespoon of oil in a non-stick pan. Add the cumin seeds and when they begin to change

colour, add the green peas, ginger, green chillies and salt, and sauté over medium heat for two minutes. Transfer to a plate and set aside to cool.

- In a large bowl, combine the cottage cheese, sautéed green peas, yam, chopped coriander, turmeric powder, *garam masala* powder, chilli powder, *chaat masala*, dried mango powder and cornflour, and mix well. Adjust the seasoning.
- Divide the mixture into sixteen equal portions and shape into lemon-sized balls. Flatten the balls lightly to form kababs.
- Heat the oil in a non-stick frying pan and shallow-fry the kababs over medium heat till golden brown. Drain on absorbent paper.
- Serve hot with green chutney.

Falafel

1 cup chickpeas

2-3 garlic cloves, chopped

A few sprigs of fresh coriander, chopped

A few sprigs of fresh parsley, chopped

4-5 stalks spring onion greens, chopped

¼ cup breadcrumbs

A small pinch of soda bicarbonate

½ teaspoon cumin powder

Salt to taste

¼ teaspoon black pepper powder

½ teaspoon paprika

Oil for deep-frying

- Wash and soak the chickpeas overnight or for at least six hours. Drain and spread on a kitchen towel to dry.
- Coarsely grind the chickpeas with the chopped garlic, chopped coriander, parsley, spring onion greens and breadcrumbs.
- Add soda bicarbonate and the cumin powder, and mix well.
- Season with salt, pepper powder and paprika. Knead the mixture well and leave to rest for a couple of hours in a refrigerator. Shape the mixture with the help of two damp tablespoons, scooping the mixture

from one tablespoon to the other till you get a uniform oval shape. Make all the falafels and store them on a greased plate in a refrigerator till ready to fry.

- Heat sufficient oil in a non-stick *kadai* and deep-fry the falafels till golden brown. Drain on absorbent paper and serve hot.

Chef's Tip

Falafels go well with tabbouleh salad and tahina dip. Falafel is traditionally made with fava beans but you can use chickpeas instead.

Chinese Bhel

200 grams eggless noodles
oil for deep-frying
2-3 spring onions, sliced
½ cup bean sprouts
¼ cup peanuts, roasted and crushed
1 tablespoon Sichuan Sauce (page 95)
1 tablespoon tomato ketchup
Sliced spring onion greens, to garnish

- Cook the noodles in six to eight cups of boiling salted water to which one tablespoon of oil has been added, till almost done. Drain, refresh in cold water, drain again and spread on a large plate to cool.
- Heat the oil in a wok and deep-fry noodles till crisp and golden brown. Drain on absorbent paper. When completely cold, lightly crush the fried noodles and set aside.
- In a large bowl, combine the fried noodles, spring onions, bean sprouts and peanuts and toss to mix well.
- Add the Sichuan sauce and tomato ketchup and toss the mixture again.
- Ladle the mixture into individual bowls or plates and serve, garnished with spring onion greens.

Achaari Idli

35-40 mini *idli*

2 tablespoons refined mustard oil

4 dried red chillies

½ teaspoon mustard seeds

¼ teaspoon fenugreek seeds

¾ teaspoon cumin seeds

½ teaspoon fennel seeds

½ teaspoon onion seeds

Salt to taste

2 tablespoons chopped fresh coriander

- Heat the mustard oil to smoking point and set aside to cool.
- Dry-roast the red chillies, mustard seeds, fenugreek seeds, cumin seeds, fennel seeds and onion seeds till fragrant. Grind to a powder; add salt and mix into the cooled mustard oil.
- Place the ground spice mixture in a non-stick pan and heat gently. Add the *idli* and toss well to mix. Serve hot, garnished with chopped coriander.

Chef's Tip

If mini *idli* are not available, you can cut regular *idli* into quarters.

Bhutta Seekh Kabab

8 pieces of baby corn, slit into two lengthways

250 grams cottage cheese

5-6 green chillies, chopped

1 teaspoon ginger-garlic paste

3 tablespoons chopped fresh coriander

1 inch ginger, chopped

1 teaspoon Kashmiri chilli powder

1 tablespoon *garam masala* powder

2 teaspoons *chaat masala*

1 teaspoon *tandoori masala*

4 bread slices, soaked and crumbled

Salt to taste

Oil for shallow-frying

- Blanch the halved pieces of baby corn in two cups of water. Drain and cool.
- Place the cottage cheese in a deep bowl and mash well. Add the green chillies, ginger-garlic paste, chopped coriander, ginger, chilli powder, *garam masala, chaat masala, tandoori masala*, bread and salt. Knead well to make a smooth dough.
- Divide the dough into sixteen portions. Shape into elongated

one-and-a-half-inch thick kabab. Insert a halved piece of baby corn into each kabab in such a way that two inches of the cob stick out.

- Heat a non-stick *tawa*. Place the kababs on it, drizzle a little oil all around and shallow-fry till golden brown. Turn the kababs over frequently so that they brown evenly.
- Serve hot with ketchup.

Chawal Ke Pakore

2 cups cooked rice

½ cup gram flour

2-3 green chillies, finely chopped

1 large onion, finely chopped

1 inch ginger, finely chopped

A few sprigs of fresh coriander, finely chopped

1 teaspoon *chaat masala*

Salt to taste

Oil for deep-frying

- Mix together all the ingredients except the oil. Add one-fourth cup of water and mix to make a thick batter.
- Heat the oil in a *kadai*. Drop spoonfuls of the batter into the hot oil and fry till light golden brown.
- Drain on absorbent paper and serve with chutney.

Hot Cheese Dip

1 cup grated processed cheese

¼ cup milk

Salt to taste

¼ teaspoon white pepper powder

¼ teaspoon dried oregano

¼ teaspoon dried thyme

- Heat the cheese and milk together in a double boiler, stirring continuously, till the cheese melts and the mixture is smooth.
- Season with salt, white pepper and dried herbs.
- Serve immediately with crudités (cut raw vegetables), wafers or bread sticks.

Chef's Tip

This dip tastes best when served hot as the cheese solidifies when cold.

Hot Hoppers

16 Bhavnagri green chillies

1 cup grated mozzarella or processed cheese

4-5 garlic cloves, peeled and chopped

1 teaspoon crushed red chillies

½ teaspoon crushed black peppercorns

2 tablespoons parsley, chopped

¾ cup refined flour

¼ cup cornflour

½ teaspoon baking powder

Salt to taste

Oil for deep-frying

- Mix together the cheese, garlic, crushed red chillies, crushed peppercorns and parsley in a bowl. Slit the chillies and remove the seeds.
- Stuff the chillies with the cheese mixture and set aside. Mix together the refined flour, cornflour, baking powder and salt in a bowl. Whisk in enough water to make a smooth, thick batter. Rest the batter for ten minutes.
- Heat the oil in a deep non-stick pan. Dip each stuffed chilli in the flour batter and deep-fry till crisp. (The chillies will not turn brown but remain white). Drain on absorbent paper and serve hot.

Corn And Bean Burritos

100 grams sweetcorn kernels

250 grams sprouted beans, blanched

4 refined flour tortillas

½ cup grated mozzarella cheese

Salt to taste

10-12 black peppercorns, crushed

1 tablespoon lemon juice

1 medium tomato, chopped

½ cup shredded lettuce

2 spring onions, chopped

2 green chillies, chopped

½ cup Salsa (page 94)

Chilled sour cream, to serve

- Preheat an oven to 200°C/400°F/ Gas Mark 6. Mix together the cheese, salt, crushed peppercorns, lemon juice and the sprouted beans in a bowl. In another bowl, mix together the tomato, lettuce and spring onions thoroughly. Add the corn and green chillies, and mix.

- Place the tortillas on a plate. Layer equal portions of the cheese and bean mixture, and the corn and tomato mixture on each tortilla. Sprinkle the salsa on top and fold each tortilla over.

- Arrange the tortillas in a baking dish and bake for twenty minutes. Serve hot with the chilled sour cream.

Kanda Bhajiya

4 large onions, sliced

Salt to taste

Oil for deep-frying

1 cup gram flour

1 teaspoon red chilli powder

- Slice the onions. Add the salt and squeeze to extract excess water.
- Heat the oil in a non-stick *kadai* till very hot.
- Add the gram flour and chilli powder to the onion and mix. Do not add any water.
- Drop portions of the onion mixture into the hot oil. If the *bhajiya* stick together, try to separate them. Drain when the *bhajiya* are half cooked.
- Just before serving, refry the *bhajiya* in very hot oil till golden brown. Drain on absorbent paper and serve hot with chutney.

Chef's Tip

Slice the onions just before frying to make crisp *bhajiya*.

Medu Vada

1 cup skinless split black gram

Salt to taste

¼ teaspoon asafoetida

8-10 curry leaves

1 teaspoon cumin powder

1 teaspoon crushed black peppercorns

Oil for deep-frying

- Wash and soak the split black gram for six hours. Grind to a fine paste.
- Add the salt, asafoetida, curry leaves, cumin powder and crushed peppercorns and mix well to make a thick batter.
- Heat the oil in a non-stick *kadai.*
- Wet the palms of your hands, and shape the batter into balls; make a hole with your thumb in the centre, like a doughnut.
- Slide the *vade* gently into the oil and deep-fry in moderately hot oil until golden brown and crisp.
- Serve hot with *sambhar* and coconut chutney.

Crusty Potato Fingers

2 large potatoes, sliced lengthways

2½ cups cornflakes, crushed

Salt to taste

Oil for deep-frying

Batter

½ cup refined flour

1 onion, roughly chopped

1 green chilli, chopped

½ inch ginger

Salt to taste

1 tablespoon cornflour

- Bring four cups of water to a boil in a pan. Add the salt and parboil the sliced potatoes. Drain and set aside.
- For the batter, grind together the onion, green chilli, ginger and salt to a fine paste.
- Mix the ground paste with the flour and cornflour. Add two tablespoons of water to make a thick batter.
- Heat sufficient oil in a non-stick *kadai.* Dip the potatoes in the batter, roll in the crushed cornflakes and deep-fry till golden. Drain on absorbent paper. Serve hot, with sauce or chutney.

Vada Pav

6 large potatoes, boiled and mashed
4 green chillies
8-10 garlic cloves
¼ teaspoon turmeric powder
A pinch of asafoetida
Juice of 1 lemon
¼ cup fresh coriander, chopped
Salt to taste
Oil for deep-frying
8 *pav*

Batter

1¼ cups gram flour
A small pinch of soda bicarbonate
¼ teaspoon turmeric powder
½ teaspoon red chilli powder
Salt to taste
1 tablespoon oil

Red Chutney

3 tablespoons grated dried coconut
2 teaspoons red chilli powder
4-6 garlic cloves
1 tablespoon oil
½ cup *besan boondi*
Salt to taste

- Grind the green chillies and garlic into a paste. Place the mashed potatoes, green chilli-garlic paste, turmeric powder, asafoetida, lemon juice, chopped coriander and salt in a bowl. Mix well.

- Divide the mixture into eight equal balls. To make the batter, mix together the gram flour, soda bicarbonate, turmeric powder, chilli powder and salt in a bowl. Heat one tablespoon of oil and stir it into the gram flour mixture. Add just enough water to make a batter of coating consistency.

- Heat sufficient oil in a non-stick *kadai.* Dip the potato balls in the batter and deep-fry till golden brown. Drain on absorbent paper.

- For the red chutney, grind together the grated coconut, chilli powder and garlic. Heat one tablespoon of oil in a non-stick pan; add the ground paste and sauté for one minute. Add the *besan boondi* and mix well. Remove from the heat and season with salt.

- Slit each *pav* horizontally, without cutting through completely. Spread the red chutney on the insides of the *pav* and stuff with hot *vada.*

- Serve hot.

Chef's Tip

With a slotted spoon, remove *besan boondi* obtained during the frying of the *vade.* Drain, cool and use in the red chutney.

Mirchi Bhajiya

8 large chillies, slit and seeded
1 cup gram flour
1 teaspoon baking powder
½ teaspoon asafoetida
1 teaspoon red chilli powder
Salt to taste
1 tablespoon oil + for deep-frying
½ teaspoon mustard seeds
4-5 garlic cloves, crushed
¼ teaspoon turmeric powder
2 large potatoes, boiled and mashed

- Whisk the gram flour, baking powder, asafoetida, chilli powder and salt with approximately one cup of water in a deep bowl to make a smooth batter. Set aside for about ten minutes.

- To make the filling, heat one tablespoon of oil in a non-stick pan and add the mustard seeds. When they begin to splutter add the crushed garlic and sauté on medium heat till fragrant.

- Add the turmeric powder and mashed potatoes, and mix well. Add the salt and mix.

- Remove from heat and set aside to cool.
- Divide the mixture into eight equal portions and stuff each chilli with a portion of the filling.
- Heat sufficient oil in a non-stick *kadai.* Dip the chillies in the gram flour batter and deep-fry till golden and crisp. Drain on absorbent paper.
- Serve hot.

Fried Garadu Indori-Style

700-800 grams *garadu*, peeled and cut into large chunks

Oil for deep-frying

2 tablespoons *Jiralu Masala* (see below)

Salt to taste

2 tablespoons lemon juice

2 tablespoons chopped fresh coriander

- Trim the narrow tapering ends of the *garadu* and use only the middle section. Grease a knife and remove the peel. Cut the *garadu* into large chunks.
- Boil seven to eight cups of water in a deep non-stick pan. Add the *garadu* chunks and boil till just done. To check for doneness, insert a knife into the thickest part of the *garadu* after six to seven minutes. If it goes in easily the *garadu* is cooked.
- Remove from heat and place in a colander to drain. Leave to cool completely.
- Chop the *garadu* into small bite-sized cubes. Heat the oil in a non-stick *kadai* over high heat. Deep-fry the *garadu* till lightly coloured. Drain on absorbent paper.

- Just before serving, refry the *garadu* in moderately hot oil till crisp. Drain on absorbent paper.
- Divide the fried *garadu* equally between serving plates, sprinkle *jiralu masala*, salt, lemon juice and chopped coriander.
- Serve immediately.

Jiralu Masala

To make *Jiralu Masala*, mix together 2 teaspoons roasted cumin powder, 1½ teaspoons dried ginger powder, ½ teaspoon red chilli powder, ¼ teaspoon turmeric powder, a pinch of asafoetida, ½ teaspoon black salt and ½ teaspoon rock salt.

Note: *Garadu is a type of yam. It is somewhat like sweet potato in appearance. You can cook any yam in this way.*

Samosa Chole

4 *samosa*

4 tablespoons yogurt, whisked

4 tablespoons Date And Tamarind Chutney (page 94)

4 tablespoons Green Chutney (page 94)

Chole

1 cup chickpeas

½ teaspoon soda bicarbonate

3 tablespoons ghee

2 medium onions, chopped

¼ cup tomato purée

1 tablespoon coriander powder

1 tablespoon cumin powder

½ tablespoon red chilli powder

Salt to taste

1 teaspoon *garam masala* powder

1 tablespoon dried mango powder

½ teaspoon black pepper powder

2 tablespoons chopped fresh coriander

- For the *chole*, soak the chickpeas overnight, or for at least six hours. Drain. Add three cups of water and half a teaspoon of soda bicarbonate to the chickpeas and cook in a pressure cooker till done.
- Heat the ghee in a non-stick pan; add the onions and sauté till pink.
- Add the tomato purée, coriander powder, cumin powder and chilli powder, and sauté again. Add the boiled chickpeas and salt. Simmer for five minutes.
- Add the *garam masala* powder, dried mango powder and pepper powder and cook for two minutes. Stir in the chopped coriander and remove from heat.
- To serve, place the *samosa* on a serving platter, crush lightly and top with a generous portion of the prepared *chole*.
- Pour the yogurt over the *chole*, drizzle with date and tamarind chutney and green chutney, and serve hot.

Surkh Tandoori Aloo

20 baby potatoes

2 tablespoons oil + for deep-frying

300 ml drained (hung) yogurt

1 tablespoon ginger-garlic paste

2 teaspoons Kashmiri red chilli paste

Salt to taste

¼ teaspoon carom seed powder

1 teaspoon *garam masala* powder

4 tablespoons roasted gram flour

2 tablespoons lemon juice

- Heat sufficient oil in a non-stick *kadai* and deep-fry the potatoes till they are half-cooked. Drain on absorbent paper and set aside.

- Place the yogurt in a bowl. Add the ginger-garlic paste, chilli paste, salt, carom seed powder, *garam masala* powder, roasted gram flour, lemon juice and two tablespoons of oil, and mix well.

- Add the fried potatoes to the marinade and mix gently. Set aside in a refrigerator to marinate for about an hour.

- Thread the potatoes a little apart onto skewers and roast in a *tandoor*.
- Alternatively, cook in an oven at 200°C/400°F/Gas Mark 6 for six to eight minutes, or till golden brown and crisp.
- Serve hot with onion *lachcha*.

Steamed Momos

1 cup refined flour

10 French beans, finely chopped

1 medium carrot, finely chopped

4-5 fresh button mushrooms, finely chopped

2 spring onions, finely chopped

¼ cup bean sprouts

8-10 cashew nuts, chopped

1 inch ginger, finely chopped

1 green chilli, finely chopped

8-10 black peppercorns, crushed

½ tablespoon light soy sauce

1 teaspoon sesame oil

¼ teaspoon MSG (optional)

Salt to taste

1 stalk spring onion greens, chopped

- Mix the refined flour with five tablespoons of water and knead into a stiff dough. Cover with a damp cloth and set aside for fifteen minutes.

- In a large bowl, combine the French beans, carrot, mushrooms, spring onions, bean sprouts, cashew nuts, ginger, green chilli, peppercorns, soy sauce, sesame oil, MSG and salt to taste.

- Divide the dough into sixteen equal portions and roll out into thin small discs.
- Place a spoonful of the vegetable filling in the centre of each disc and bring the sides together in the centre, pinching firmly together to form a dumpling.
- Line a steamer with a clean, damp piece of muslin and arrange the momos in it.
- Cover and steam for eight to ten minutes, until the momos are cooked through.
- Transfer to a serving plate. Garnish with spring onion greens and serve hot with Sichuan Sauce (page 95).

Kand Ke Pattice

500 grams purple yam, boiled and grated

2 medium potatoes, boiled and grated

Salt to taste

½ cup grated coconut

5-6 black peppercorns, crushed

7-8 cashew nuts, finely chopped

2 green chillies, chopped

½ inch ginger, chopped

1 tablespoon raisins

1 tablespoon chopped fresh coriander

1 cup arrowroot powder

Oil for deep-frying

- Grate the yam and potato in separate bowls, add salt to each and knead till smooth.
- To make the stuffing, mix together the coconut, crushed peppercorns, cashew nuts, green chillies, ginger, raisins and salt in a bowl. Add the chopped coriander and mix.
- Take a small portion of the mashed potato, roll lightly in arrowroot powder and pat it into a small disc on your palm.
- Place a portion of the filling, gather up the edges and roll into a ball.

- Take a portion of the mashed yam, roll lightly in arrowroot powder and pat it into a slightly larger disc on your palm.
- Place the stuffed potato ball in the centre, gather up the edges and roll into a ball. Place it in a mould, press lightly, unmould and set it aside on a plate. You can make the patties in advance and place in a refrigerator to deep-fry them just before serving.
- Heat sufficient oil in a deep non-stick pan. Sprinkle some arrowroot powder over the patties so that the shape is retained.
- Gently slide them into the hot oil and deep-fry on medium heat till crisp and lightly browned. Drain on absorbent paper.
- Serve hot with sweetened yogurt or Green Chutney (page 94).

Missal Pav

8 *pav*

1 cup sprouted green gram

1 cup sprouted brown gram

2 tablespoons oil

A pinch of asafoetida

½ teaspoon mustard seeds

A few curry leaves

2 large onions, finely chopped

2 green chillies, slit

1 teaspoon garlic paste

1 teaspoon ginger paste

½ teaspoon turmeric powder

1½ teaspoons red chilli powder

1 teaspoon coriander-cumin powder

Salt to taste

1 teaspoon *garam masala* powder

2 tablespoons fresh coriander, finely chopped

½ cup *farsan*

Lemon juice, as required

Lemon wedges, as required

- Mix the sprouted gram in a colander and wash under running water for one minute. Drain. Heat the oil in a non-stick pan; add the asafoetida, mustard seeds, curry leaves and half the onions. Sauté for one minute and add the green chillies, garlic paste and ginger paste. Stir well and sprinkle a little water.

- Add the turmeric powder, chilli powder and coriander-cumin powder. Mix well and add the sprouted gram. Add salt to taste and three cups of water and bring to a boil. Add the *garam masala* powder and chopped coriander, reserving some for garnishing. Cover and cook for ten to twelve minutes.

- To serve, place a ladleful of cooked sprouted gram in each small, deep bowl. Sprinkle generously with *farsan*. Sprinkle the remaining onion, remaining chopped coriander and the lemon juice over the *farsan*. Serve with lemon wedges and *pav*.

Moong Dal Cheela

1¼ cups split green gram with skin
1½ inches ginger, roughly chopped
5-6 garlic cloves, roughly chopped
1 medium onion, roughly chopped
3 green chillies, roughly chopped
Salt to taste
¼ teaspoon red chilli powder
Oil, as required
¾ cup Green Chutney (page 94)
¾ cup cottage cheese, grated

- Soak the gram in three cups of water for about half an hour. Drain and grind with the ginger, garlic, onion, green chillies and salt to make a smooth batter.
- Add the chilli powder and mix well. Heat a non-stick *tawa* and grease it with oil. Spread a ladleful of batter with the back of the ladle into a thin round.
- Drizzle a little oil and cook on medium heat till the underside is cooked. Carefully flip the *cheela* over, drizzle a little oil and cook the other side too. Spread some green chutney over the *cheela*. Sprinkle the cottage cheese and fold the *cheela* over into a half-moon shape. Serve hot.

Annexure

Date And Tamarind Chutney

Wash, stone and chop 15-20 dates. Dry-roast 2 teaspoons cumin seeds and ¼ teaspoon fennel seeds. Cool and grind to a powder. Cook the dates, 1 cup tamarind pulp, cumin and fennel powder, ½ cup jaggery, 2 teaspoons red chilli powder, 1 teaspoon dried ginger powder, black salt, salt and four cups of water till thick.

Green Chutney

Grind together 1 cup fresh coriander, ½ cup fresh mint, 2-3 green chillies, black salt to taste, ¼ teaspoon sugar and 1 tablespoon lemon juice to a smooth paste using a little water if required.

Red Chilli-Garlic Chutney

Soak 10 red chillies in 1½ cups of water for half an hour. Drain and grind with 12 large garlic cloves and 2 teaspoons lemon juice to a fine paste. Add sea salt and 1 teaspoon cumin powder and mix well.

Salsa

Roast 2 halved large onions, 5 halved garlic cloves, 4 halved medium tomatoes and 1 quartered capsicum on a hot griddle till the skins are charred. Cool and grind coarsely with salt. Transfer to a bowl and stir in the lemon juice.

Sichuan Sauce

Boil 10-12 dried red chillies in 1 cup of water for 5 to 7 minutes. Drain, cool and grind to a fine paste. Heat ½ cup oil in a pan; add 10 finely chopped garlic cloves, 2 finely chopped green chillies, 2 finely chopped spring onions and 1 inch ginger, grated, and sauté for 1 minute. Add the red chilli paste and sauté for a few more seconds. Add 2-3 inches celery stalk, finely chopped, 3 tablespoons tomato ketchup and salt to taste, and stir well to mix. Stir in 2 teaspoons white vinegar and simmer for 1 minute till the oil rises to the surface. Cool and store.

Note: *Sichuan sauce will keep for 1 month if there is sufficient oil covering the surface.*

Tamarind Pulp

Soak 75 grams tamarind in 100 ml warm water for 10-15 minutes. Grind to a smooth paste and strain to remove any fibres. Store in an airtight container in the refrigerator.

Vegetable Stock

Peel, wash and chop 1 onion, ½ medium carrot, 2-3 inch celery stalk and 2-3 garlic cloves. Place in a pan with 1 bay leaf, 5-6 peppercorns, 2-3 cloves and 5 cups of water and bring to a boil. Lower heat and simmer for 15 minutes and strain. Cool and store in a refrigerator till further use.

Wonton Wrappers

Knead 2 cups of refined flour with ½ cup warm water to make a firm dough. Roll the dough into a large thin square sheet, about 1 mm thick. Cut into 3-inch squares and use as required.

Glossary

English	Hindi
Almonds	Badam
Asafoetida	Hing
Bean sprouts	Ankurit moong
Bottle gourd	Doodhi
Butter	Makkhan
Capsicum	Shimla mirch
Cardamom, green	Chhoti elaichi
Cashew nuts	Kaju
Chickpeas	Kabuli chana
Cinnamon	Dalchini
Cloves	Laung
Coconut, dried	Khopra
Coriander seeds	Dhania
Coriander, fresh	Hara dhania
Cottage cheese	Paneer
Cumin seeds	Jeera
Fennel seeds	Saunf
Fenugreek seeds	Methidana
Gram flour	Besan
Gram, black skinless split	Dhuli urad dal
Gram, brown	Matki
Gram, green	Sabut moong
Gram, split green	Chilkewali moong dal
Mango, unripe, dried and powdered	Amchur
Mushroom	Khumb
Mustard seeds	Rai
Nutmeg	Jaiphal
Onion seeds	Kalonji
Peanuts	Moongphali
Peppercorns, black	Kali mirch
Pigeon peas, split	Arhar dal/toovar dal
Raisins	Kishmish
Refined flour	Maida
Saffron	Kesar
Sago	Sabudana
Spinach	Palak
Spring onion	Hara pyaaz
Spring onion greens	Hare pyaaz ke patte
Vinegar	Sirka
Yam	Zamikand/suran
Yogurt	Dahi